PEEL + DISCOVER®

SPACE

Welcome to your Peel + Discover activity book!

Inside are hundreds of stickers of all things outer space—from Jupiter to the International Space Station!

But this is a sticker book unlike any other: Once you've peeled off all the stickers, you'll discover cool facts about space underneath. Create a book that's all your own as you sticker, color, and draw on all the activity pages. Ever wonder what weird things humans have sent to space or how many asteroids are in the asteroid belt? If so, then this is the book for you!

3 . . . 2 . . . 1 . . . →

Library of Congress Cataloging-in-Publication Data is available.

ISBN 978-1-5235-0874-7

Designed by Claire Torres
Illustrations by Bolaji Olaloye

Workman books are available at special discounts when purchased in bulk for premiums and sales promotions as well as for fund-raising or educational use. Special editions or book excerpts can also be created to specification. For details, contact the Special Sales Director at the address below, or send an email to specialmarkets@workman.com.

Workman Publishing Co., Inc.
225 Varick Street
New York, NY 10014-4381
workman.com

WORKMAN and PEEL+DISCOVER are registered trademarks of Workman Publishing Co., Inc.

Printed in China
First printing April 2020

10 9 8 7 6 5 4 3 2 1

blastoff!

To get to outer space, we need a spacecraft with powerful rockets to lift us beyond Earth's atmosphere. American space shuttles had rocket boosters that reached speeds of up to 18,000 mph!

Quick! Color this space shuttle as it launches into outer space!

our solar system

Our solar system has 8 planets that rotate around the Sun. Ours is one of many solar systems that make up a galaxy called the Milky Way. Our solar system revolves around the center of the Milky Way, called the Galactic Bulge. Scientists think the bulge could be a black hole.

The Milky Way Galaxy

Scutum-Centaurus Arm

Orion Arm

Perseus Arm

Sun

Galactic Bulge

The Milky Way is a spiral galaxy with different "arms" where groups of stars, planets, and solar systems can be found. Our solar system is in the tiny Orion Arm.

JUPITER

VENUS

EARTH

MOON

MERCURY

MARS

SUN

URANUS

SATURN

NEPTUNE

Peel me up!

the planets

If you need to remember the order of the planets from closest to farthest from the Sun, just use this saying: **M**y **V**ery **E**nthusiastic **M**other **J**ust **S**erved **U**s **N**oodles!

Can you put the planets in order using the saying above? HINT: The planet closest to the Sun is Mercury!

so many moons!

Earth has only 1 moon—some planets have many, and others have none at all. Our solar system has over 190 moons of all shapes, sizes, and materials, from rock to solid ice.

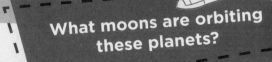

What moons are orbiting these planets?

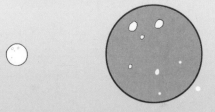

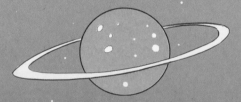

astronauts

Astronauts are people (or animals!) who travel beyond the limits of the Earth's atmosphere and do research in outer space. Some astronauts have walked on the Moon, while others have spent time in shuttles or living at the International Space Station.

Space Milestones!

First Dog to Orbit Earth
Laika, 1957

First Person in Space
Yuri Gagarin, 1961

First Woman in Space
Valentina Tereshkova, 1963

First Person on the Moon
Neil Armstrong, 1969

First All-Female Space Walk
Christina Koch and Jessica Meir, 2019

MARK AND SCOTT KELLY

KATHERINE JOHNSON

SPACE SUIT

SALLY RIDE

NASA

HAM THE ASTROCHIMP

LELAND MELVIN

NEIL ARMSTRONG

MAE JEMISON

BUZZ ALDRIN

Peel me up!

zero gravity

Gravity is the invisible force that pulls objects toward a planet's surface. In outer space, the pull of gravity is much weaker, so when astronauts are living in shuttles or on space stations, they—and anything else that isn't tied down—float! Pencils, food, water . . . anything!

What is floating in this spaceship?

m00n walk

In 1969, Neil Armstrong and Buzz Aldrin became the first people to walk on Earth's Moon. Since then, 10 more people have walked on the Moon—including Alan Shepard, who snuck golf balls and club onto the shuttle and hit shots on the Moon!

What is this astronaut doing on the Moon?

spaceCraft

The universe is so gigantic that almost all of it is too far away for humans to travel to—at least for now. That's why scientists send machines like probes, satellites, rovers, and telescopes to collect information, conduct experiments, and explore all the places in space they can't reach.

How Much Does It Weigh?

Weight depends on gravity. Because the Earth's gravity is stronger, objects are heavier on Earth than they are on the Moon. Here is what these spacecraft weigh:

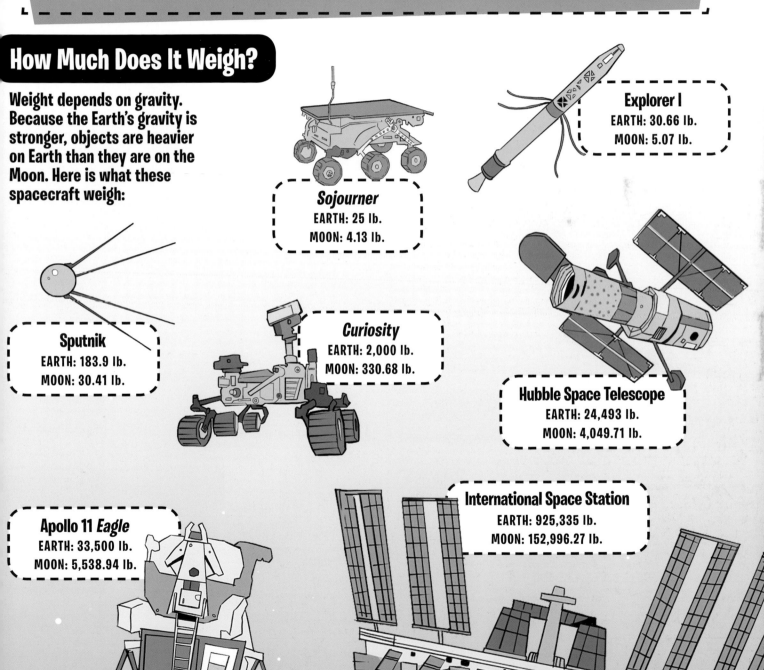

Sojourner
EARTH: 25 lb.
MOON: 4.13 lb.

Explorer I
EARTH: 30.66 lb.
MOON: 5.07 lb.

Sputnik
EARTH: 183.9 lb.
MOON: 30.41 lb.

Curiosity
EARTH: 2,000 lb.
MOON: 330.68 lb.

Hubble Space Telescope
EARTH: 24,493 lb.
MOON: 4,049.71 lb.

Apollo 11 _Eagle_
EARTH: 33,500 lb.
MOON: 5,538.94 lb.

International Space Station
EARTH: 925,335 lb.
MOON: 152,996.27 lb.

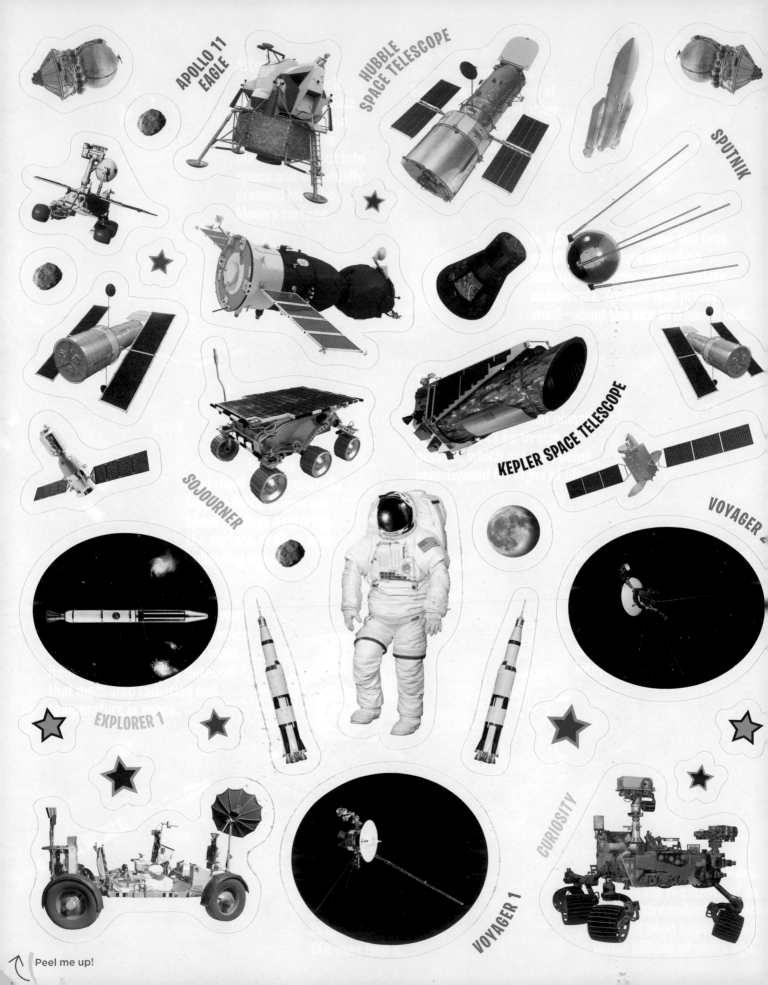

APOLLO 11 EAGLE

HUBBLE SPACE TELESCOPE

SPUTNIK

SOJOURNER

KEPLER SPACE TELESCOPE

VOYAGER 2

EXPLORER 1

CURIOSITY

VOYAGER 1

Peel me up!

mission to mars

Humans haven't been to Mars yet, but they have sent robots called rovers to explore the planet's surface. Mars is the only other planet in our solar system with the potential for life, and astronauts are eager to learn if humans can survive there.

Can this rover find clues to life on Mars?

far out!

A space probe is any spacecraft sent to space to conduct research without a human. This includes rovers, satellites that orbit a specific planet, and machines that travel great distances and snap pictures of what they see.

Where are these probes headed?

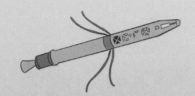

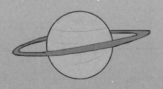

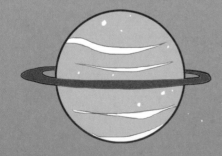

what's up there?

Our solar system has more floating around in it than just planets and moons. Some things are natural, like asteroids, comets, and meteors. Others are things humans have put up there or left behind—like telescopes, probes, and even a car!

Weird Things We've Sent to Space

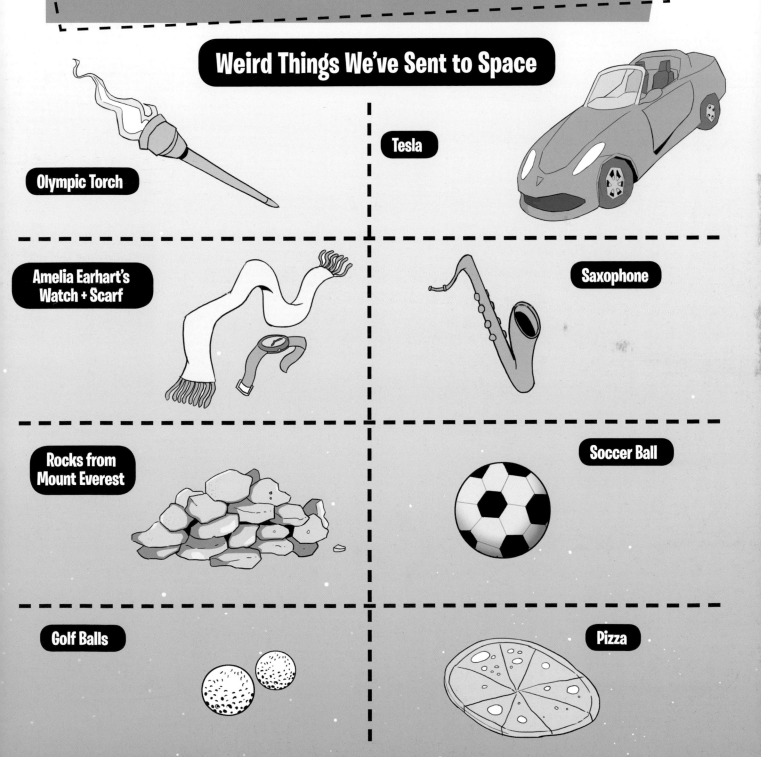

Olympic Torch

Tesla

Amelia Earhart's Watch + Scarf

Saxophone

Rocks from Mount Everest

Soccer Ball

Golf Balls

Pizza

METEORS

PLUTO

SUPERNOVA

AURORA

STARS

ASTEROID

HALLEY'S COMET

NEBULA

BLACK HOLE

GALAXY

Peel me up!

crash landing!

So many objects travel through space that sometimes they collide—with each other and with planets! These collisions create more space debris, which ends up in orbit or leaves crater marks on the surface of planets.

What's crashing around in outer space?

asteroid belt

The asteroid belt is an area between Mars and Jupiter where most of the asteroids in our solar system orbit the Sun. There are millions of asteroids in the asteroid belt, but if you put them all together, they would weigh less than Earth's moon.

The asteroid belt has asteroids of all shapes and sizes. Add some wacky-looking asteroids here!

stargazing

The night sky has always been a source of wonder for scientists and poets alike. For most of history, humans were unable to leave Earth to explore space. Instead, they collected all the data they could about the appearance of the night sky and the movement of the Moon, stars, planets, and the Sun to understand what is up there.

Lunar Phases

First Quarter

Waxing Gibbous

Waxing Crescent

Waning Gibbous

Full

New

Earth

Waning Crescent

Third Quarter

Sun

The Moon is always round, but we can see only the part that's lit up by the Sun. That's why the Moon seems to change shape in the sky.

ECLIPSE

SOUTHERN CROSS

SUPERMOON

CANIS MAJOR

TELESCOPE

SEXTANT

OBSERVATORY

KECK I AND II

RADIO TELESCOPE

constellations

Constellations are groups of stars that, when connected, sometimes look like animals, creatures, or familiar things. Early navigators used the constellations to find their way as they explored.

Connect the stars to reveal the constellations!

Ursa Major

5
2 3 4 6
1
7

Southern Cross

Ursa Minor
1
2
3
4
7 5
6

Scorpius

Cassiopeia

stargazers

An astronomer is a scientist who studies the universe beyond Earth. In 1609, Galileo Galilei became the first astronomer to study space from Earth using a telescope. He saw craters and mountains on the Moon and observed the Milky Way.

What can the astronomer see through her telescope?

space travel

NASA has sent many different types of craft into space. Here are the ones that carried humans.

NASA's Major Missions

PROJECT MERCURY

1958-1963

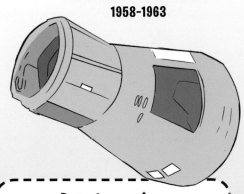

GOAL: Put a human in space

SPACECRAFT: Mercury spacecraft

PROJECT APOLLO

1968-1972

GOAL: Put first person on the Moon

SPACECRAFT: Apollo 11 Command and Service Module

THE SPACE SHUTTLE PROGRAM

1981-2011

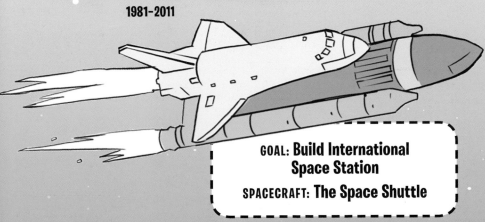

GOAL: Build International Space Station

SPACECRAFT: The Space Shuttle

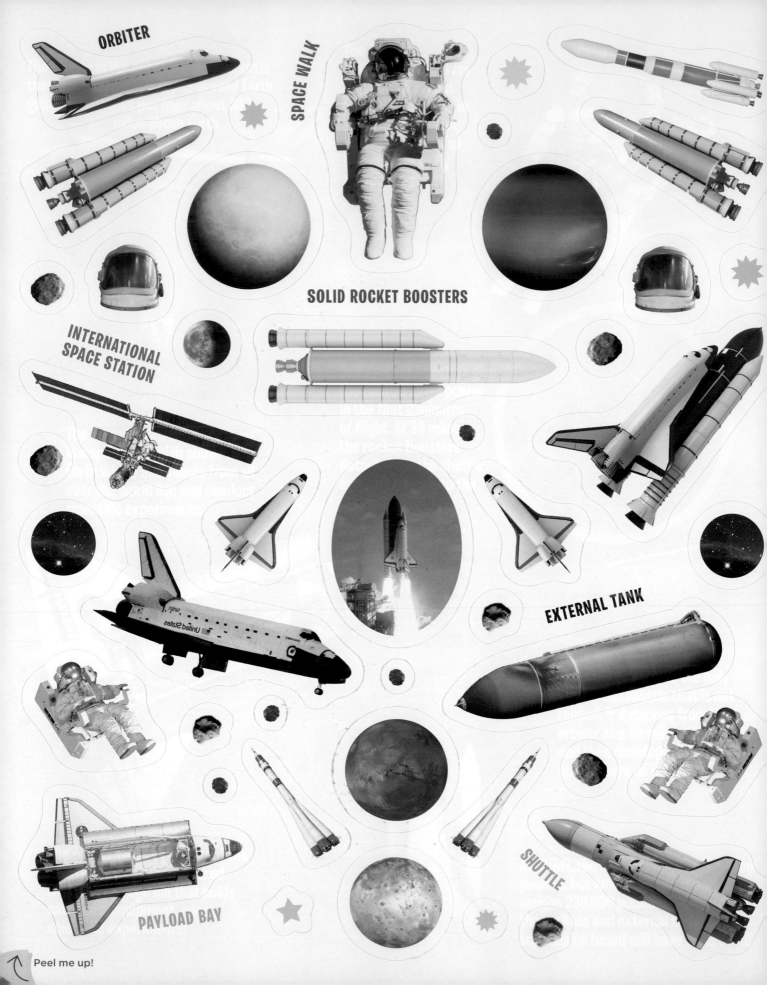

ORBITER

SPACE WALK

SOLID ROCKET BOOSTERS

INTERNATIONAL SPACE STATION

EXTERNAL TANK

SHUTTLE

PAYLOAD BAY

Peel me up!

let's go to space!

When astronauts go to space, they are often headed for the International Space Station. There, astronauts sometimes go on space walks to repair broken satellites, conduct experiments, and test the effects of being in space.

Who else is going on this space walk?

what's out there?

Even with all of their research, scientists understand only about 5 percent of the universe. The other 95 percent is made up of what scientists call dark matter and dark energy, which still remain a mystery.

What do you think dark energy could be?